To my students –

The depth in which you observe,
is the extent of what you will know.
The more you create,
the further humanity will go.

Life's Little Project Books is a TM of GenBeam LLC.
© 2019 by GenBeam, LLC.
Book, cover and internal design by GenBeam LLC.
Cover and internal illustrations © 2019 by GenBeam, LLC.
Published in the United States by GenBeam, LLC.
All rights reserved.

For questions and bulk orders, please contact us at
genbeamllc@gmail.com

Life's Little Project Books believes in capturing life's little nuggets to better ourselves, humanity, and pass on the knowledge to our future generations.

Inventor's Disclosure Notebook

Inventor Name: _____

Contact Number: _____

---

*Guided Notebook for
Patent Applications, Licensing Technology,
Business Ideas, and Investor Pitches*

INTRODUCTION

WHAT ARE INVENTION DISCLOSURES

Invention disclosures are the first step to identify intellectual property and determining how to proceed with it. Intellectual property may be patented, licensed, or commercialized as part of a start-up. This notebook is to help you capture your ideas, identify what's new and useful that's been invented, and to help you think about how you want to proceed.

BEST KNOWN METHODS

These are tips on making your invention stronger.

REFRAIN FROM INITIAL PATENT SEARCHES

When you have an idea, let it nurture and grow to allow for original solutions to surface. Many times, inventors start doing patent searches right away, allowing for a wall of doubt to spring up. This can severely inhibit your creative development phase. Patent searches are important, but be sure to give yourself time to develop your idea to an invention before external solutions take over. When doing market research, use '-patent' in Google, to filter out these results. Some companies don't allow their employees to conduct patent searches. Check with the legal department or review company policies to confirm.

HAVE A TEAM OF CO-INVENTORS

Working in teams with diverse backgrounds, genders, and experiences can strengthen your invention. This value can come in the form of new usage cases, unique component modifications, and methods of reaching the target customer. Larger teams can lead to chaos and confusion on who the inventors actually are. A lone inventor misses out on alternative perspectives which brings value to the invention. 2-6 people seems an optimal number, but this can vary depending on your specific situation.

SEEK FEEDBACK FROM 3-5 EXPERIENCED INVENTORS

Seeking advice from experienced inventors can add value to your invention. It's not uncommon for the person providing feedback to offer a new inventive elements, which would likely make them a co-inventor if you decide to include their contribution. Many times these inventors can tell you what's already been done, but what may also be unique about your solution.

COMPLETE DRAFT INVENTION DISCLOSURE WITHIN 1-2 MONTHS

When developing an idea into an invention, timeliness is important. There are numerous situations to make you think your idea is not good enough. As fast as you can, draft your idea into an invention disclosure. Let it simmer for 1-2 months while you seek feedback and work with your co-inventors to revise.

ALLOW FOR CROSS-POLLINATION

Working on several ideas in parallel can allow creative and original solutions to pollinate between seemingly unrelated ideas. This can also happen by engaging in discussions with people outside your field of expertise or by engaging in diverse hobbies.

STEPS AFTER SUBMITTING INVENTION
Suggestions to partake after you have submitted your idea for review.

WHILE YOU WAIT
Once you file an invention disclosure, depending on your situation, you should continue to take action. This may include working on the next invention disclosure, digging into market research, prototyping and surveying the marketplace, filing for a trademark, or conducting deeper research into the best way to monetize. What you don't want to do is sit idle. It can take a long time to go from an idea to a patent being granted. If you submit a patent application to the Patent and Trademark Office, your product becomes 'patent pending'.

WHEN A COMPANY SAYS DO NOT FILE
If you are submitting your invention to your companies IP group as an employee, many times they will come back with a Do Not File recommendation, also known as a DNF. It is common for an inventor to receive rather little details as to why, which can leave you with lots of questions and discouragement. Seek out a meeting with the portfolio manager to understand why. This is a valuable exercise to get feedback with the IP portfolio manager, and to also ensure the invention disclosure wasn't misunderstood. In some cases, you may apply for a release, which would allow you to take the invention out of your employer to file on your own. State legislature and company policies need to be considered.

FINDING COMPANIES FOR LICENSING
Many companies seek ideas from external sources to bring fresh ideas into their product lines. This is known as the open innovation platform and has been gaining steam for the last 10 years. Most big companies partaking in these programs require at least a provisional patent. This is an inexpensive way to claim ownership for your invention before investing thousands of dollars in actual utility or design patents.

PROTOTYPING
Having a working model of your invention can help you think through the caveats of the idea. If drawing on the white board and talking out loud about the key aspects of the invention is not enough, a prototype may help. However, keep the prototype simple and inexpensive. If you can mock it up within a week, it's a good initial prototype. Don't let perfectionism sacrifice the timeliness.

INCREASING YOUR SUCCESS RATE
The more ideas you develop, the better you will become at having good, original ideas that are valuable to the marketplace. A good way to increase your success rate is to increase the quantity of ideas you develop into inventions. These invention disclosures then need to be submitted to the Patent & Trademark Office. Lots of inventors lose steam once their invention is drafted, and never submit. This limits your learning and feedback you receive on the other end. As you generate more ideas to inventions, your inventorship skills will increase. After filing one invention, take a break, and start on the next one.

BRAIN DUMP
List out all the ideas you have for inventions and products.
Tip: Think about problems in your daily life to inspire you.

IDEA #	IDEA	PAGE
1		
2		
3		
4		
5		
6		
7		
8		
9		
10		
11		
12		
13		
14		
15		
16		
17		
18		
19		
20		
21		
22		
23		
24		
25		

Select your favorite top 10 ideas to explore further in the following pages.

IDEA #	IDEA	PAGE
26		
27		
28		
29		
30		
31		
32		
33		
34		
35		
36		
37		
38		
39		
40		
41		
42		
43		
44		
45		
46		
47		
48		
49		
50		

INTRODUCTION

DESCRIPTIVE INVENTION TITLE
(Title clearly describing what the invention does)

NAMES OF THE INVENTORS
List the names of the inventors and their contact information

_____   _____
_____   _____
_____   _____

OBJECT OF INVENTION
1-2 sentences describing a use or function of the invention.
Ex: "The purpose of the invention is to catch mice."

_____
_____
_____
_____
_____

HOW DID YOU COME UP WITH THE IDEA?

_____
_____
_____
_____
_____
_____
_____

Date: _____   Location: _____

BACKGROUND INFORMATION

DESCRIPTION OF PROBLEM(S) SOLVED OR IMPROVED BY INVENTION
What problem did you solve? How did you identify the problem(s)?

PREVIOUS SOLUTION(S)
What solutions exist and why don't they solve your problem?

OVERVIEW OF THE INVENTION

BRIEF DESCRIPTION OF INVENTION (3-5 SENTENCES)
Please highlight the features of your solution.
Explain if your solution a method, a device, or a design and how it works.

_____
_____
_____
_____
_____
_____
_____
_____
_____

ADVANTAGES AND BENEFITS OF INVENTION
Describe its value to your company, customers, and the world.
What makes your invention unique or better than the competition?
Is your invention compatible with existing products in the industry?

_____
_____
_____
_____
_____
_____
_____
_____
_____
_____

USE CASES
Identify the different use cases for your invention and your target audience.

MARKET
Identify the different markets your invention would be used in
Ex: education, niche markets, military, industry, service, or healthcare.

DETAILS OF THE INVENTION

FIGURE 1
Draw a high-level, bird's-eye, view of the invention.
Use flow diagrams, graphs, or other data to illustrate the invention.

FIGURE 1 EXPLANATION
Describe the different components of your invention illustrated in Figure 1.

FEEDBACK

Asking feedback from trusted, diverse, and experienced sources can help strengthen your ideas. Seek 2-10 people to get feedback on your ideas. Ex: potential end-users, experts, patent attorneys, connections in marketing, connections in publishing, etc.

ADDITIONAL FEEDBACK, SKETCHES OR NOTES

FIGURE 2
Draw a process flow-diagram on how the invention operates or functions. Indicate what part of the invention already exists, and what part of the invention you feel is new. Ex: use blue = existing, green = new

FIGURE 2 EXPLANATION
Describe the different components of your invention illustrated in Figure 2.

COMMERCIALIZATION INFORMATION

AWARENESS
How will the market become aware of your product? What is the cost?

GENERATING REVENUE
How do you or your company propose to capitalize on your product?
Ex: license, online retail, third-party, or use as defense patent.

COMPETITION
Who is your competition?

TARGET CUSTOMER
Describe the target customer.
Identify shopping habits and how they spend their time.

INTRODUCTION

DESCRIPTIVE INVENTION TITLE
(Title clearly describing what the invention does)

NAMES OF THE INVENTORS
List the names of the inventors and their contact information

_____   _____
_____   _____
_____   _____

OBJECT OF INVENTION
1-2 sentences describing a use or function of the invention.
Ex: "The purpose of the invention is to catch mice."

_____
_____
_____
_____
_____

HOW DID YOU COME UP WITH THE IDEA?

_____
_____
_____
_____
_____
_____
_____

Date: _____   Location: _____

BACKGROUND INFORMATION

DESCRIPTION OF PROBLEM(S) SOLVED OR IMPROVED BY INVENTION
What problem did you solve? How did you identify the problem(s)?

PREVIOUS SOLUTION(S)
What solutions exist and why don't they solve your problem?

OVERVIEW OF THE INVENTION

BRIEF DESCRIPTION OF INVENTION (3-5 SENTENCES)
Please highlight the features of your solution.
Explain if your solution a method, a device, or a design and how it works.

___

ADVANTAGES AND BENEFITS OF INVENTION
Describe its value to your company, customers, and the world.
What makes your invention unique or better than the competition?
Is your invention compatible with existing products in the industry?

___

USE CASES
Identify the different use cases for your invention and your target audience.

MARKET
Identify the different markets your invention would be used in
Ex: education, niche markets, military, industry, service, or healthcare.

DETAILS OF THE INVENTION

FIGURE 1
Draw a high-level, bird's-eye, view of the invention.
Use flow diagrams, graphs, or other data to illustrate the invention.

FIGURE 1 EXPLANATION
Describe the different components of your invention illustrated in Figure 1.

FEEDBACK

Asking feedback from trusted, diverse, and experienced sources can help strengthen your ideas. Seek 2-10 people to get feedback on your ideas. Ex: potential end-users, experts, patent attorneys, connections in marketing, connections in publishing, etc.

ADDITIONAL FEEDBACK, SKETCHES OR NOTES

FIGURE 2
Draw a process flow-diagram on how the invention operates or functions. Indicate what part of the invention already exists, and what part of the invention you feel is new. Ex: use blue = existing, green = new

FIGURE 2 EXPLANATION
Describe the different components of your invention illustrated in Figure 2.

COMMERCIALIZATION INFORMATION

AWARENESS
How will the market become aware of your product? What is the cost?

GENERATING REVENUE
How do you or your company propose to capitalize on your product? Ex: license, online retail, third-party, or use as defense patent.

COMPETITION
Who is your competition?

TARGET CUSTOMER
Describe the target customer.
Identify shopping habits and how they spend their time.

INTRODUCTION

DESCRIPTIVE INVENTION TITLE
(Title clearly describing what the invention does)

NAMES OF THE INVENTORS
List the names of the inventors and their contact information

OBJECT OF INVENTION
1-2 sentences describing a use or function of the invention.
Ex: "The purpose of the invention is to catch mice."

HOW DID YOU COME UP WITH THE IDEA?

Date: Location:

BACKGROUND INFORMATION

DESCRIPTION OF PROBLEM(S) SOLVED OR IMPROVED BY INVENTION
What problem did you solve? How did you identify the problem(s)?

PREVIOUS SOLUTION(S)
What solutions exist and why don't they solve your problem?

OVERVIEW OF THE INVENTION

BRIEF DESCRIPTION OF INVENTION (3-5 SENTENCES)
Please highlight the features of your solution.
Explain if your solution a method, a device, or a design and how it works.

_____

ADVANTAGES AND BENEFITS OF INVENTION
Describe its value to your company, customers, and the world.
What makes your invention unique or better than the competition?
Is your invention compatible with existing products in the industry?

_____

USE CASES
Identify the different use cases for your invention and your target audience.

MARKET
Identify the different markets your invention would be used in
Ex: education, niche markets, military, industry, service, or healthcare.

DETAILS OF THE INVENTION

FIGURE 1
Draw a high-level, bird's-eye, view of the invention.
Use flow diagrams, graphs, or other data to illustrate the invention.

FIGURE 1 EXPLANATION
Describe the different components of your invention illustrated in Figure 1.

FEEDBACK

Asking feedback from trusted, diverse, and experienced sources can help strengthen your ideas. Seek 2-10 people to get feedback on your ideas. Ex: potential end-users, experts, patent attorneys, connections in marketing, connections in publishing, etc.

ADDITIONAL FEEDBACK, SKETCHES OR NOTES

FIGURE 2
Draw a process flow-diagram on how the invention operates or functions. Indicate what part of the invention already exists, and what part of the invention you feel is new. Ex: use blue = existing, green = new

FIGURE 2 EXPLANATION
Describe the different components of your invention illustrated in Figure 2.

COMMERCIALIZATION INFORMATION

AWARENESS
How will the market become aware of your product? What is the cost?

GENERATING REVENUE
How do you or your company propose to capitalize on your product? Ex: license, online retail, third-party, or use as defense patent.

COMPETITION
Who is your competition?

TARGET CUSTOMER
Describe the target customer.
Identify shopping habits and how they spend their time.

INTRODUCTION

DESCRIPTIVE INVENTION TITLE
(Title clearly describing what the invention does)

NAMES OF THE INVENTORS
List the names of the inventors and their contact information

_____   _____
_____   _____
_____   _____

OBJECT OF INVENTION
1-2 sentences describing a use or function of the invention.
Ex: "The purpose of the invention is to catch mice."

_____
_____
_____
_____
_____

HOW DID YOU COME UP WITH THE IDEA?

_____
_____
_____
_____
_____
_____

Date: _____   Location: _____

BACKGROUND INFORMATION

DESCRIPTION OF PROBLEM(S) SOLVED OR IMPROVED BY INVENTION
What problem did you solve? How did you identify the problem(s)?

PREVIOUS SOLUTION(S)
What solutions exist and why don't they solve your problem?

OVERVIEW OF THE INVENTION

BRIEF DESCRIPTION OF INVENTION (3-5 SENTENCES)
Please highlight the features of your solution.
Explain if your solution a method, a device, or a design and how it works.

_____
_____
_____
_____
_____
_____
_____
_____
_____

ADVANTAGES AND BENEFITS OF INVENTION
Describe its value to your company, customers, and the world.
What makes your invention unique or better than the competition?
Is your invention compatible with existing products in the industry?

_____
_____
_____
_____
_____
_____
_____
_____
_____
_____

USE CASES
Identify the different use cases for your invention and your target audience.

MARKET
Identify the different markets your invention would be used in
Ex: education, niche markets, military, industry, service, or healthcare.

DETAILS OF THE INVENTION

FIGURE 1
Draw a high-level, bird's-eye, view of the invention.
Use flow diagrams, graphs, or other data to illustrate the invention.

FIGURE 1 EXPLANATION
Describe the different components of your invention illustrated in Figure 1.

FEEDBACK

Asking feedback from trusted, diverse, and experienced sources can help strengthen your ideas. Seek 2-10 people to get feedback on your ideas. Ex: potential end-users, experts, patent attorneys, connections in marketing, connections in publishing, etc.

ADDITIONAL FEEDBACK, SKETCHES OR NOTES

FIGURE 2
Draw a process flow-diagram on how the invention operates or functions. Indicate what part of the invention already exists, and what part of the invention you feel is new. Ex: use blue = existing, green = new

FIGURE 2 EXPLANATION
Describe the different components of your invention illustrated in Figure 2.

COMMERCIALIZATION INFORMATION

AWARENESS
How will the market become aware of your product? What is the cost?

GENERATING REVENUE
How do you or your company propose to capitalize on your product? Ex: license, online retail, third-party, or use as defense patent.

COMPETITION
Who is your competition?

TARGET CUSTOMER
Describe the target customer.
Identify shopping habits and how they spend their time.

INTRODUCTION

DESCRIPTIVE INVENTION TITLE
(Title clearly describing what the invention does)

NAMES OF THE INVENTORS
List the names of the inventors and their contact information

_____   _____
_____   _____
_____   _____

OBJECT OF INVENTION
1-2 sentences describing a use or function of the invention.
Ex: "The purpose of the invention is to catch mice."

_____
_____
_____
_____
_____

HOW DID YOU COME UP WITH THE IDEA?

_____
_____
_____
_____
_____
_____

Date: _____   Location: _____

BACKGROUND INFORMATION

DESCRIPTION OF PROBLEM(S) SOLVED OR IMPROVED BY INVENTION
What problem did you solve? How did you identify the problem(s)?

PREVIOUS SOLUTION(S)
What solutions exist and why don't they solve your problem?

OVERVIEW OF THE INVENTION

BRIEF DESCRIPTION OF INVENTION (3-5 SENTENCES)
Please highlight the features of your solution.
Explain if your solution a method, a device, or a design and how it works.

ADVANTAGES AND BENEFITS OF INVENTION
Describe its value to your company, customers, and the world.
What makes your invention unique or better than the competition?
Is your invention compatible with existing products in the industry?

USE CASES
Identify the different use cases for your invention and your target audience.

MARKET
Identify the different markets your invention would be used in
Ex: education, niche markets, military, industry, service, or healthcare.

DETAILS OF THE INVENTION

FIGURE 1
Draw a high-level, bird's-eye, view of the invention.
Use flow diagrams, graphs, or other data to illustrate the invention.

FIGURE 1 EXPLANATION
Describe the different components of your invention illustrated in Figure 1.

FEEDBACK

Asking feedback from trusted, diverse, and experienced sources can help strengthen your ideas. Seek 2-10 people to get feedback on your ideas. Ex: potential end-users, experts, patent attorneys, connections in marketing, connections in publishing, etc.

ADDITIONAL FEEDBACK, SKETCHES OR NOTES

FIGURE 2

Draw a process flow-diagram on how the invention operates or functions. Indicate what part of the invention already exists, and what part of the invention you feel is new. Ex: use blue = existing, green = new

FIGURE 2 EXPLANATION
Describe the different components of your invention illustrated in Figure 2.

COMMERCIALIZATION INFORMATION

AWARENESS
How will the market become aware of your product? What is the cost?

GENERATING REVENUE
How do you or your company propose to capitalize on your product? Ex: license, online retail, third-party, or use as defense patent.

COMPETITION
Who is your competition?

TARGET CUSTOMER
Describe the target customer.
Identify shopping habits and how they spend their time.

INTRODUCTION

DESCRIPTIVE INVENTION TITLE
(Title clearly describing what the invention does)

NAMES OF THE INVENTORS
List the names of the inventors and their contact information

_____   _____
_____   _____
_____   _____

OBJECT OF INVENTION
1-2 sentences describing a use or function of the invention.
Ex: "The purpose of the invention is to catch mice."

_____
_____
_____
_____
_____

HOW DID YOU COME UP WITH THE IDEA?

_____
_____
_____
_____
_____
_____

Date: _____   Location: _____

BACKGROUND INFORMATION

DESCRIPTION OF PROBLEM(S) SOLVED OR IMPROVED BY INVENTION
What problem did you solve? How did you identify the problem(s)?

PREVIOUS SOLUTION(S)
What solutions exist and why don't they solve your problem?

OVERVIEW OF THE INVENTION

BRIEF DESCRIPTION OF INVENTION (3-5 SENTENCES)
Please highlight the features of your solution.
Explain if your solution a method, a device, or a design and how it works.

___

ADVANTAGES AND BENEFITS OF INVENTION
Describe its value to your company, customers, and the world.
What makes your invention unique or better than the competition?
Is your invention compatible with existing products in the industry?

___

USE CASES
Identify the different use cases for your invention and your target audience.

MARKET
Identify the different markets your invention would be used in
Ex: education, niche markets, military, industry, service, or healthcare.

DETAILS OF THE INVENTION

FIGURE 1
Draw a high-level, bird's-eye, view of the invention.
Use flow diagrams, graphs, or other data to illustrate the invention.

FIGURE 1 EXPLANATION
Describe the different components of your invention illustrated in Figure 1.

FEEDBACK

Asking feedback from trusted, diverse, and experienced sources can help strengthen your ideas. Seek 2-10 people to get feedback on your ideas. Ex: potential end-users, experts, patent attorneys, connections in marketing, connections in publishing, etc.

ADDITIONAL FEEDBACK, SKETCHES OR NOTES

FIGURE 2
Draw a process flow-diagram on how the invention operates or functions. Indicate what part of the invention already exists, and what part of the invention you feel is new. Ex: use blue = existing, green = new

FIGURE 2 EXPLANATION
Describe the different components of your invention illustrated in Figure 2.

COMMERCIALIZATION INFORMATION

AWARENESS
How will the market become aware of your product? What is the cost?

GENERATING REVENUE
How do you or your company propose to capitalize on your product? Ex: license, online retail, third-party, or use as defense patent.

COMPETITION
Who is your competition?

TARGET CUSTOMER
Describe the target customer.
Identify shopping habits and how they spend their time.

INTRODUCTION

DESCRIPTIVE INVENTION TITLE
(Title clearly describing what the invention does)

NAMES OF THE INVENTORS
List the names of the inventors and their contact information

_____   _____
_____   _____
_____   _____

OBJECT OF INVENTION
1-2 sentences describing a use or function of the invention.
Ex: "The purpose of the invention is to catch mice."

_____
_____
_____
_____
_____

HOW DID YOU COME UP WITH THE IDEA?

_____
_____
_____
_____
_____
_____

Date: _____   Location: _____

BACKGROUND INFORMATION

DESCRIPTION OF PROBLEM(S) SOLVED OR IMPROVED BY INVENTION
What problem did you solve? How did you identify the problem(s)?

PREVIOUS SOLUTION(S)
What solutions exist and why don't they solve your problem?

OVERVIEW OF THE INVENTION

BRIEF DESCRIPTION OF INVENTION (3-5 SENTENCES)
Please highlight the features of your solution.
Explain if your solution a method, a device, or a design and how it works.

ADVANTAGES AND BENEFITS OF INVENTION
Describe its value to your company, customers, and the world.
What makes your invention unique or better than the competition?
Is your invention compatible with existing products in the industry?

USE CASES
Identify the different use cases for your invention and your target audience.

MARKET
Identify the different markets your invention would be used in
Ex: education, niche markets, military, industry, service, or healthcare.

DETAILS OF THE INVENTION

FIGURE 1
Draw a high-level, bird's-eye, view of the invention.
Use flow diagrams, graphs, or other data to illustrate the invention.

FIGURE 1 EXPLANATION
Describe the different components of your invention illustrated in Figure 1.

FEEDBACK

Asking feedback from trusted, diverse, and experienced sources can help strengthen your ideas. Seek 2-10 people to get feedback on your ideas. Ex: potential end-users, experts, patent attorneys, connections in marketing, connections in publishing, etc.

ADDITIONAL FEEDBACK, SKETCHES OR NOTES

FIGURE 2
Draw a process flow-diagram on how the invention operates or functions. Indicate what part of the invention already exists, and what part of the invention you feel is new. Ex: use blue = existing, green = new

FIGURE 2 EXPLANATION
Describe the different components of your invention illustrated in Figure 2.

COMMERCIALIZATION INFORMATION

AWARENESS
How will the market become aware of your product? What is the cost?

GENERATING REVENUE
How do you or your company propose to capitalize on your product? Ex: license, online retail, third-party, or use as defense patent.

COMPETITION
Who is your competition?

TARGET CUSTOMER
Describe the target customer.
Identify shopping habits and how they spend their time.

INTRODUCTION

DESCRIPTIVE INVENTION TITLE
(Title clearly describing what the invention does)

NAMES OF THE INVENTORS
List the names of the inventors and their contact information

OBJECT OF INVENTION
1-2 sentences describing a use or function of the invention.
Ex: "The purpose of the invention is to catch mice."

HOW DID YOU COME UP WITH THE IDEA?

Date: Location:

BACKGROUND INFORMATION

DESCRIPTION OF PROBLEM(S) SOLVED OR IMPROVED BY INVENTION
What problem did you solve? How did you identify the problem(s)?

PREVIOUS SOLUTION(S)
What solutions exist and why don't they solve your problem?

OVERVIEW OF THE INVENTION

BRIEF DESCRIPTION OF INVENTION (3-5 SENTENCES)
Please highlight the features of your solution.
Explain if your solution a method, a device, or a design and how it works.

ADVANTAGES AND BENEFITS OF INVENTION
Describe its value to your company, customers, and the world.
What makes your invention unique or better than the competition?
Is your invention compatible with existing products in the industry?

USE CASES
Identify the different use cases for your invention and your target audience.

MARKET
Identify the different markets your invention would be used in
Ex: education, niche markets, military, industry, service, or healthcare.

DETAILS OF THE INVENTION

FIGURE 1
Draw a high-level, bird's-eye, view of the invention.
Use flow diagrams, graphs, or other data to illustrate the invention.

FIGURE 1 EXPLANATION
Describe the different components of your invention illustrated in Figure 1.

FEEDBACK

Asking feedback from trusted, diverse, and experienced sources can help strengthen your ideas. Seek 2-10 people to get feedback on your ideas. Ex: potential end-users, experts, patent attorneys, connections in marketing, connections in publishing, etc.

ADDITIONAL FEEDBACK, SKETCHES OR NOTES

FIGURE 2
Draw a process flow-diagram on how the invention operates or functions. Indicate what part of the invention already exists, and what part of the invention you feel is new. Ex: use blue = existing, green = new

FIGURE 2 EXPLANATION
Describe the different components of your invention illustrated in Figure 2.

COMMERCIALIZATION INFORMATION

AWARENESS
How will the market become aware of your product? What is the cost?

GENERATING REVENUE
How do you or your company propose to capitalize on your product?
Ex: license, online retail, third-party, or use as defense patent.

COMPETITION
Who is your competition?

_____
_____
_____
_____
_____
_____

TARGET CUSTOMER
Describe the target customer.
Identify shopping habits and how they spend their time.

_____
_____
_____
_____
_____
_____
_____
_____
_____
_____
_____
_____
_____
_____
_____
_____

INTRODUCTION

DESCRIPTIVE INVENTION TITLE
(Title clearly describing what the invention does)

NAMES OF THE INVENTORS
List the names of the inventors and their contact information

_____   _____
_____   _____
_____   _____

OBJECT OF INVENTION
1-2 sentences describing a use or function of the invention.
Ex: "The purpose of the invention is to catch mice."

_____
_____
_____
_____
_____

HOW DID YOU COME UP WITH THE IDEA?

_____
_____
_____
_____
_____
_____

Date: _____   Location: _____

BACKGROUND INFORMATION

DESCRIPTION OF PROBLEM(S) SOLVED OR IMPROVED BY INVENTION
What problem did you solve? How did you identify the problem(s)?

PREVIOUS SOLUTION(S)
What solutions exist and why don't they solve your problem?

OVERVIEW OF THE INVENTION

BRIEF DESCRIPTION OF INVENTION (3-5 SENTENCES)
Please highlight the features of your solution.
Explain if your solution a method, a device, or a design and how it works.

ADVANTAGES AND BENEFITS OF INVENTION
Describe its value to your company, customers, and the world.
What makes your invention unique or better than the competition?
Is your invention compatible with existing products in the industry?

USE CASES
Identify the different use cases for your invention and your target audience.

___

MARKET
Identify the different markets your invention would be used in
Ex: education, niche markets, military, industry, service, or healthcare.

DETAILS OF THE INVENTION

FIGURE 1
Draw a high-level, bird's-eye, view of the invention.
Use flow diagrams, graphs, or other data to illustrate the invention.

FIGURE 1 EXPLANATION
Describe the different components of your invention illustrated in Figure 1.

FEEDBACK

Asking feedback from trusted, diverse, and experienced sources can help strengthen your ideas. Seek 2-10 people to get feedback on your ideas. Ex: potential end-users, experts, patent attorneys, connections in marketing, connections in publishing, etc.

ADDITIONAL FEEDBACK, SKETCHES OR NOTES

FIGURE 2
Draw a process flow-diagram on how the invention operates or functions. Indicate what part of the invention already exists, and what part of the invention you feel is new. Ex: use blue = existing, green = new

FIGURE 2 EXPLANATION
Describe the different components of your invention illustrated in Figure 2.

COMMERCIALIZATION INFORMATION

AWARENESS
How will the market become aware of your product? What is the cost?

GENERATING REVENUE
How do you or your company propose to capitalize on your product? Ex: license, online retail, third-party, or use as defense patent.

COMPETITION
Who is your competition?

TARGET CUSTOMER
Describe the target customer.
Identify shopping habits and how they spend their time.

INTRODUCTION

DESCRIPTIVE INVENTION TITLE
(Title clearly describing what the invention does)

NAMES OF THE INVENTORS
List the names of the inventors and their contact information

_____   _____
_____   _____
_____   _____

OBJECT OF INVENTION
1-2 sentences describing a use or function of the invention.
Ex: "The purpose of the invention is to catch mice."

_____
_____
_____
_____
_____

HOW DID YOU COME UP WITH THE IDEA?

_____
_____
_____
_____
_____
_____

Date: _____   Location: _____

BACKGROUND INFORMATION

DESCRIPTION OF PROBLEM(S) SOLVED OR IMPROVED BY INVENTION
What problem did you solve? How did you identify the problem(s)?

PREVIOUS SOLUTION(S)
What solutions exist and why don't they solve your problem?

OVERVIEW OF THE INVENTION

BRIEF DESCRIPTION OF INVENTION (3-5 SENTENCES)
Please highlight the features of your solution.
Explain if your solution a method, a device, or a design and how it works.

___

ADVANTAGES AND BENEFITS OF INVENTION
Describe its value to your company, customers, and the world.
What makes your invention unique or better than the competition?
Is your invention compatible with existing products in the industry?

___

USE CASES
Identify the different use cases for your invention and your target audience.

MARKET
Identify the different markets your invention would be used in
Ex: education, niche markets, military, industry, service, or healthcare.

DETAILS OF THE INVENTION

FIGURE 1
Draw a high-level, bird's-eye, view of the invention.
Use flow diagrams, graphs, or other data to illustrate the invention.

FIGURE 1 EXPLANATION
Describe the different components of your invention illustrated in Figure 1.

FEEDBACK

Asking feedback from trusted, diverse, and experienced sources can help strengthen your ideas. Seek 2-10 people to get feedback on your ideas. Ex: potential end-users, experts, patent attorneys, connections in marketing, connections in publishing, etc.

ADDITIONAL FEEDBACK, SKETCHES OR NOTES

FIGURE 2
Draw a process flow-diagram on how the invention operates or functions. Indicate what part of the invention already exists, and what part of the invention you feel is new. Ex: use blue = existing, green = new

FIGURE 2 EXPLANATION
Describe the different components of your invention illustrated in Figure 2.

COMMERCIALIZATION INFORMATION

AWARENESS
How will the market become aware of your product? What is the cost?

GENERATING REVENUE
How do you or your company propose to capitalize on your product? Ex: license, online retail, third-party, or use as defense patent.

COMPETITION
Who is your competition?

TARGET CUSTOMER
Describe the target customer.
Identify shopping habits and how they spend their time.

Don't Stop

"on average, creative geniuses weren't qualitatively better in their fields than their peers. They simply produced a greater volume of work, which gave them more variation and a higher chance of originality."

— Adam M. Grant
Originals: How Nonconformists Move the World

Life's Little Project Books Library

amazon.com/author/LifesLittleProjectBooks

Made in the USA
Middletown, DE
20 January 2022